FORBIDDEN PLUMS

POEMS IN QUARANTINE BY
Peggy Dobreer

GLASS LYRE PRESS

Copyright © 2021 Peggy Dobreer
Paperback ISBN: 978-1-941783-76-4

All rights reserved: Except for the purpose of quoting brief passages for review, no part of this book may be reproduced or transmitted in any form or by any means, electronic or mechanical, including photocopying, recording, or by any information storage and retrieval system, without permission in writing from the publisher.

Design & Layout: Steven Asmussen
Cover art: 'Untitled (Venus with Virus, 2020)' by Brendan Constantine

Glass Lyre Press, LLC
P.O. Box 2693
Glenview, IL 60025
www.GlassLyrePress.com

Forbidden Plums

(Poems from the first 40 days of quarantine, 2020)

ACKNOWLEDGMENTS

Every book of poetry is a collaboration of inspiration, skill, and permission which assembles into a whole much greater than the poems alone. The following contributions to this book have made it possible. I am grateful beyond measure to:

~Ami Kaye, Publisher of Glass Lyre Press and the entire Glass Lyre staff for their vision and for giving this young manuscript a home.

~Steven Asmussen, Managing Editor & Layout Designer at Glass Lyre Press for creativity, guidance, flexibility, and patience in 'building the bones' of this book.

~Brendan Constantine, poet, teacher, collaborator, author of "Dementia, my Darling" for cover art collage and more: "Untitled (Venus with Virus, 2020)" made from Titian's 'Venus with a Mirror,' oil on canvas circa 1555 and a colorized electron micrograph of an apoptotic cell (green) heavily infected with SARS-COV-2 virus particles (purple). Image captured and color enhanced at NIAID Integrated Research Facility (IRF) in Fort Derrick, Maryland.

~Juanita Davis, writer, workshop collaborator for language in 'Red Feathers Flocking.'

~Mandy Kahn, author of Glenn Gould's Chair, Poet-in-Residence at The Los Angeles Philosophical Research Society where "Love Song to San Francisco" was taped in performance for "PEACE."

~Janet Fitch, author of *Chimes of a Lost Cathedral, The Revolution of Marina M.* and *White Oleander* for kind words and ongoing inspiration.

~Chad Sweeney, author of *Little Million Doors, Parable of Hide and Seek*, and *Arranging the Blaze* for Zoom tutelage and generous comments.

~ Lois P. Jones, author of *Night Ladder*, for many contributions to my poetry life and glorious comments on the cover of *Forbidden Plums*.

~Sallie & Ed Raspa, in whose spare room these poems were written.

Thank You.

"THERE is wisdom in this; beyond the rules of physic: a man's own observation, what he finds good of, and what he finds hurt of, is the best physic to preserve health."

—*Francis Bacon*

"LET us read and let us dance; these two amusements will never do any harm to the world."

—*Voltaire*

Contents

Acknowledgments   v

Part I
The Shock of Exception

Tine & Promise	1
Crossings	2
Phantom in Sight	3
On the Second Day	4
Of a Middle Temper	5
Newborn	6
The Elephant in the Tent	7
Mourning the Dead	8
Even If We Started Near the End…	10
St. Anthony Takes a Bow	11
On the Wheel	13
The Glistening	14
Technique	15
Moxibustion	16

Entries:
Untoward Symmetry

I. Vicissitudes	19
II. Inquisition	20
III. Discords	21
IV. Distant Motion	22
V. Simulation	23
VI. Trust	24
VII. Giddied Up	25

Chapter Two
Oscillant Entrainment

At William's Old Desk	29
Impossibly Unloving Him	30
Sternum	31
Fool's Gold in the Eyes of Love	32
What You Can't See, You Can't See.	33
Sometime this Century	34
Forbidden Plums…	35
Time, like a River, Flows Away	36
Red Feathered Flock	37
Painted Ladies & Pants	38
Gathered Safely In	41
About the Author	45

*for my dear
Brendan, Janet and Perla*

Part I

The Shock of Exception

Tine & Promise

When the wax has been pulled
and filed to a shape most
pleasing to the carver's hand.

When the kiln is fired and
flask set dead center. When
heat rounds the silken core

and in those first few hours,
the mold does ooze and
grimace, roasting away from

the unforgiving glare, we sneak
a look and waves peel across
the studio. Green folds into

carbon black on steel, armature,
burst and sizzle, bites of time,
hiss and song of industry.

Then the latch is unhinged,
tongs grab clumsy, mittened
hand. Torch is lit. Crucible brought

to the self-same heat for the pour. The
steady draw, vacuum pump pulls metal
ring ward. Empty channels fill to sprue.

Then water hits the rim, and white cylinder
goes calcium stream. The yet dull golden gift
plunks the sink, unpolished tine and promise.

Crossings

I carry death like respite. Like
one last chance at anything
untainted by imminent annihilation.

Everyone has changed their tone.

Come-uppance is now required for
compliance, mandatory testing is reliance.
No one left standing will be left standing.

When two and two add up to a baker's
dozen, absence on the backburner
simmers into bone done broth.

Some trees require cross-pollination.
Others volunteer between cracks in asphalt.
They don't care.

Just as your face shimmers in my slip,
a boat drifts — like a crab at the dock.
The lake holds fewer and fewer trout.
The sea never flavors upstream.

O, tributaries, deliver us to the other.
The fractured hub, less thumper with every
slight proffered, with every un-met vetting.

Phantom in Sight

Awakened by machines starting
up in the corner of the room.

Apparitions are closer now. Serenaded
by rain awning toward my window.

More power to the polls, love of country gone
viral. Sheets of holy heaven sent

sideways toward the glass, leaping forward
without resolve for every error wrought.

There is no view through a glass darkly.
There is no invitation to unshelter in place.

This separated scandal of missed
marks and unwed shores. It wriggles

in restrictions imposed. Whatever leap
I might have made rests in a messy nest

of whiskered birds. Clouds gone quiet
in billows and striations. I will miss this

forever if I pass in seclusion, roomed in a safety
that swallows me full. The chords

between us tighten with every flight. Every
closed door, each elbowed elevator peg.

This is a virus I won't survive one more time.
But I wonder why I don't just play my last hand

and let myself go out like that, with all my missed
marks bundled into one last straw.

ON THE SECOND DAY

Sometimes the right thing is to watch

snow melt or wait on leaves to drop.

If you listen intent, they frack on the wind

like young folks with cell phones. You

are not young, but your heart is a child.

Your power animal, a stuffed bear from

your favorite immigrant aunt who smells

of mothballs and *kreplach*. There is a time

to hunker way down. Let the back of your

neck speak to the drapes in your mind.

Or hum when your too tired to speak.

Desire croons to the wick of arrested flames

OF A MIDDLE TEMPER

And furthermore...you don't
have to go to Gethsemane
on every point. A hair's
breadth is just a hair's breadth.
An inch is simply an inch.
Need not become a mile.
Don't construct elegy. Don't
make mythical proportion
of some small synchronicity.
Listen with your skin and bone.
Ears have so little purpose
in the hunger of the heart.
Your power source cannot
be renewed in this position.
Pawn your indecision for
whatever you can get.
Be no more patient. Be
whole in your singularity.
Rest at the crest of nothingness.
Your nothingness is everything.
Everything begins again at go.

NEWBORN
poem to honor U.S. first responders

The cranial arc is tender at birth.
See the way first steps mimic dancing,

the way *piques* in a row are a small forest,
light streaming across southern exposure,

a wish to the north end of a coral reef.
Extremophile caving is dangerous sport.

Only adults are allowed to jump out of planes.
A young girl with crossed legs and a fear

of heights paces the grainy sky while clouds
gather and hell breaks out in New York City.

A doctor is forced to choose for God and
we can't stand in allegiance to that. Singing

last rites sheds mercy from nurses who
have left the womb for the eastern coast.

The Elephant in the Tent

When you say what you say
with your buttons undoing
for pennies on the dollar,
the ringmaster will suddenly spit
his teeth from atop the only elephant
in the tent. When she foals, she dies.

The gray calf, given the name Tobias,
is taken out and staked to the ground
by a chain the length of a half sentence,
twice the price of admission, but if he
strays from the stake, it tugs at his ankle
leaving scars the size of the Kalahari.

By the time his weight is vast enough to
unstake the spike, he conditions that he
hasn't the strength to free himself. So,
instead, remains a prisoner of his own
deception until rused in lock and chain
he's led back to the tent, decked in frills
and palanquin to let clowns run ram shot
around his trunk, just as they did his mother.

Mourning the Dead

The bones of saints should
not be buried. But poured
over like an elephant clan,

gristled with the charge of a
herdsman. A fallen skeleton,
dried gray hide, black eye, weight

of trunk and tusk. The carriage
of head and horn, of ears furrowing,
hooves closing in on remains

of the perished calf. It is the
lady herd that comes first,
the milk of primary knowing.

On a womb lowered knee,
the matriarch scans the field,
herd now cloven, now

severed upon them. What is
to be known, asked, measured?
What sway might come to dance

this sacred interrogation? What
was made here, fouled from
the pack? No packed burial.

No pyre. Only the passing of
winds. Saints delivered unto the sky
set open for fouling weather,

for flood or snowfall, parchment
or silt. Saints cannot be left to lie
still. Their task is their nature. No

question can be left. The elephants
scan the fallen, the drawn away.
They take their time. It takes as long
as it takes. Three days, maybe more.

Even If We Started Near the End...

we'd most likely be here till a pair of spooked horses
ended up in the canal. That is to say, until the date
groves needed heating to keep the fruit from freezing.

That is to say, things got set in motion long before gears
began to grind. The very fact she has gotten away with
smiling all these years is perhaps most egregious of perjuries.

No one is to blame. She abandoned balconies for back stairs,
rooftops for the front seat of a tin nickel. Everything else
was chigger pale. Contradictions that would cause Sartre

or Kierkegaard to set forth an honest inquiry. There'd be
no leaping ahead. Ten cents apiece. Dance cards would
be signed, signatures would fail. The rules can sure slap

like birthmarks across the face of each fresh idea. Would
you care for chocolates or icicles before we go? Can you
help us chart a way from this despair?

St. Anthony Takes a Bow

I'm holding out hope
for a garnet ring of stars.

I should know better,
dreamer that I am.

Nightmare seeker
in the dark of Isis.

I'm holding out
like a freak in

king's clothing.
Like a naked draper

at the window, washing
for spring in the dead

of summer. The
sun beats the sky with

wolfing carnage and
hawk's blood soup.

If someone you have
never met meets you

in a hotel lobby, run
like a dandelion in

high water pants and mini
skirts. Tell what you were

wearing, admissible in
court. Let the morning flux

wash your own wither
back to you. Let it simmer

in sludge from your city
streets, your time sunken

cheeks. We all sink
beneath the drainage

of our longing, if we
live long enough.

If St. Anthony will
only crown our heads

with thorns and veritas,
if the punk headed

bulbuls make a nest
beneath our sorrows,

wake us at dawn, chirp
nice to meet you, nice to

meet you...well then, shoo
them away and get on.

On the Wheel

The moment when vision and craft marry...
that makes you keep coming back, keep coming back,
keep coming back to poetry.
—Kwame Dawes

There is clay in our palms,
each and only unto the potter.
We have been engraved with
fractals of functional brilliance.
What I mean is the whole *magila*.
That any two of these many billion
could occupy this complexity, this
locus of passion, tunnels of inequity.

And yes it cannot roll downhill.
How in love we hide and swap
hours with dawn, make a wing
of our wish, a beacon of terror,
our haunted melody.

You can blame this apocalypse on
my obligation to tenderness. So,
a pony trumps a horse any day,
a field of geese fly against a violet scrim,
black magic erupts from the firestorm,
from the risen living shift of us.
Till there is no *now* left to risk.

THE GLISTENING
after "Things I Didn't Know I Loved" by Nazim Hikmet

I didn't know I loved the wide arms of the plum, holding
her fruit 'til plunging below late summer. I didn't know
I loved the dull wooden fence that plaited my secret cove.
I didn't know I loved Chinatown at three A.M. Herbs and
roots, fish eyes and steam, pungent in windows.

I didn't know I loved the slender heads of Modigliani's
women, their brains elongated by his keen sense of line.
I didn't know I loved the rhonunculus patch in front of the
art museum, Shakespearean sonnets out on the avenues.

I knew I loved the freedom, the Presidio, and the most lovely
harp made from the jawbone of a whale. And I knew I would be
happy with no less. So, I road cable cars when I needed redress,
ate raw salmon on Fisherman's Wharf, oysters off tiles at Swan's,
and chips drowned in vinegar on Polk Street.

But who would have guessed I would come to love rain, walking
till drenched in the keen emerald eye of a twinkling Marina Green.

Technique

A dancer walks down Mission Street
with a Marlboro in one hand, a latte
from La Boheme in the other. A rainbow
muffler wrapped around thorax,

warming calves, pumping smoke,
dragging deep into the celery snap of
another San Francisco morning and
itching to pull on the day's first leotard.

This is Mariposa, heart of the dance.
A cable car up Polk, bus across town,
stop at the café and finally hoofing it
into the warehouse district.

Industrial doors open to cement
hallways, to studio spaces softened
by sprung wood floors. The smell
of kiln and oil paint, and the long push

of a cotton broom across caramel colored
floors. Always care of the floor comes first.
Breath falls to lower chakras, dissolves all
dissonance. And light streams in through

southern exposure. Today, the spirit of
Erick Hawkins wields the broom. Footsteps
are a barely audible imprint on the ear,
so quiet you can hear your breath.

And a five, six, seven and eight.

Moxibustion

Dr. Foon was an expert in butterfly harps and reading
pulses. The deeper tones of the body guided his potions.

Needles became embedded without puncturing skin.
He could sense the space between cells.

The subtleties of harp are intricacies of wind. The way
hammers fall onto strings by the play of wing and gravity.

It is ever in the falling, in the seconds of air before landing.

If a woman dies at the helm of a craft, is it a comfort to he who
loved her, that the winter sky was clear and as ancient as her longing?

The things we love cross us over, give way to radiance, like white
hot shimmer off a silver strand that blinds the tumbler, splitting seconds,

changing light so sheering it cannot be contained. When her sternum
was fractured and pressed on her chest, Foon sat her up. Said to lean

forward, letting the hammer of her breastbone fall away from
the bulk of her heart, wounded muscle, fractured leap.

Be of the airtime, the flight and fall. Take heed
of landing, once it's happened, it's happened.

Roots and herbs simmer down
in a cast iron pot on an open flame.

Entries:
Untoward Symmetry

I. Vicissitudes

Who's there? I ask aloud. You say nothing, turn your glance, glaze over. I can see by your shield that your home is north of the range behind us. I see the sterling in your beard, the hull of your frame and the suffering behind your third eye. I mark the distance you have come on foot by the wear on your moccasins and the smell of bear on your neck.

II. Inquisition

I don't know where I lost the way of
extending invitations. I stopped
fixing curried lamb, lighting wicks.
No longer selected sparkling wines,
taking time and pomp to pour at the
table. I've stopped the spin of a decent
music source in my room. Unless I
hum. And how can I hum and converse at
once? This sore dilemma. I don't know at
what juncture this distemper first showed
up. Can't map the slow descent into stasis.
Impasses impale my spirit bear.

III. Discords

The taste of creme brulé without coffee is
very much like the sound of a voice in my
ear without the ear close enough to taste.
Where we land next is undetermined, like
solar orbit, as much a surprise as the
ringing in my head when silence becomes
too great for my room to contain. When I
pan the folds in the drapes, threads between
our chests become entangled for more, for
the too much to carry, the too snug to fit,
too slow to keep current with the river on
its way through night banks of treason and
silt.

IV. Distant Motion

The same smell of bear in print. A trail of scuffs along the sedges. Our howling to the other, terminal to terminal. My eyes open into sweat gathering in your shoulder pools, giving way to your pumper against mine. Your hands brace my back, its arching reach to lay my selves on your cheek. Your eyes look wet, as though we had been crying. I reach in my purse for a hanky, but you are miles to go before you sleep, and other arrangements have to keep. Keep your distance, if nothing else, at all cost.

V. SIMULATION

Wandering pages of an old journal I land
on the slant of a southpaw. One of which,
I am not whom. I search between letters,
beyond punctuation, inside thoughts that
brought me here before the pencil took the
page. Before the ink dried. Before
lustrations leapt into view. Once hidden
vowels have made headlines in the company
of the right consonants on Hollywood Blvd.
Saturday night isn't close to the hook of
your arm under my neck, or the weight of
your head on my chest. I love bubbles and
bargains, and the color of apricots. I'm not
fancy and don't even mention children.
Some things go simple and long as you
knit.

VI. Trust

Like a cabled sweater from Ireland, worn more often over the years by the moths in the closet than by the weaver herself. Let go such a sweater. Give it to the man in the wheelchair who looks cold. Let go the sweater, your wings, and the blouse that hugs them. Twirl your skirts around the meadow, poppies are beginning to bloom.

VII. Giddied Up

The web of confine wobbles like planets turning in place, knitting up the cosmos in flattening the curve and pace. Saturn has undressed her rings and Mars has shed a moon. Orion's belt is bitten bloody in the teeth of a brash red dog, and the Ursas have turned tail and run from the family of sky. Nothing as it was is how it now goes. It goes slowly, threatened by inertia, and more slowly now at warp speed.

Chapter Two

Oscillant Entrainment

At William's Old Desk
"I have woven a parachute out of everything broken."

—William Stafford

I.
The salt of this. What it quenches.

II.
The way he handles a hardback of Jane Kenyon.
His open hand receives her spine. My back opens
in response, like a psalm whispered through each
vertebra, root to crown. His attention unzips
our prologue.

III.
Prince of time, he captures and coerces
the juices of observation from my palms. I
prepare food like sacrament. The nighthare
buries a fallen doe in a grove of maple shards.

IV.
There is no four on the Fibonacci trail.

V.
I transform to mushroom, mulch, mountain. I
have given you many children. Can you name one
between us? For you I spin and trance. Tell me all
my children are beautiful. Watch me bear your fruit.

VI.
We are 70,000 words of love strong. We are verb
and noun. We dare birthing modifiers. Most changes
disqualify others. We are not contradictions. We are
two power animals, interspecies play in the wild. We
sleep briefly in the arms of the wondrous, the fallen,
feared and restored.

Impossibly Unloving Him

See. This is what it does
                        not come to.

Neither added up or abled aloft
                        even for later exile.

A languid tide rolls in. Only
                        one road to land's end, along

an extravagance of savage cliffs.
                        This unheartening from

ledges emblazoned with
                        unsung moons in her hair.

A dirge of every breaker
                        tossed against a sea wall

whisks them around in
                        a clutch of clouds.

STERNUM

We could call it prison bone,
fortifies the cage of the chest.

We could call it flat fish on shore,
heaving at every rush of prana,

its tentacles spread wide as windmills
anchored behind splayed wings. We

could call it flower of the middle road.
Gladiolus in the hand of the heart,

convex from clavicle to xyphoid,
an unpaired plate known to nest

the muscles of flight in birds. O,
how we fly out now, landing harder

every time. I lay the white bone
over mine, snuggle it between

our daughters. My heart beats
against it. Here's a voice, my

weak contrition. *Softly*, it says. *Say it
again, more softly. Say sternum.*

*Like you're holding me down with a slow
silver spoon, sailing the swells of my storm.*

Fool's Gold in the Eyes of Love
after "Skin" by Dr. Richard Selzer

This is my body, this house of peril,
"sac to tote my runny vitals grave ward,
first playground, last prison." Cellmate
of loss and drum, scars of mind lapses,
slip and falls. Garden of veritas and light,
you plant my coarsened chamber, a germ so
deep, it won't be washed by rain or snow.

Your sleet of restraint, seeds of hope where
none were sown, where nothing before spread
such suchness in bright full tones. You hold me
in places unknown and familiar. Your pitched
grace gaveled. Gentle and floweredy fulcrum.
May it break over me like dawn's gloried spark
like a gemstone in a day's quandried fervor.

This is my body, invisible acre, moon lander,
cold star of stars coming out on this dark
Corona, this black depth of coal shaft, kettle
bottom thunker, once leaf hewn and shade
provoking, provider, now boom lowered,
calling our courage back. Flesh and chant,
rutilated breath, delicate provider, insider
and long left out.

What You Can't See, You Can't See.

Right between the who-ras and righty-ohs.
Outback by the whitewashed fence and
the moon in Cancer. Reflected in the ripples
on the lake. Sore losers and right well-winners.

If you listen closely, there is one true sound
like a baby laughing. It grips and loosens,
comes like an avalanche of joy. Like lovers
gasping for a song, while the ice shelf melts
or gets hung above the larder for spices and herbs.

If a rabbit pulls your eyes out of the hat,
you will witness multi facets of time, and
preferences of the unseen will shift shape
into life force.

The existential Easter hunt is a long line
from Sunday, and when we all come clear,
the grass in the basket will stop its neon hue,
nest eternity in its lyrical sphere. No one
will fake weep at this leaving. No one
will squeeze the cat just to make him cry.

Sometime this Century

A mood ring watered
at the shore. The last
time I wore it with that
dress, color of blue tide,
electric shimmer. The
cellular sound of Velella,
Velella, whispering.

Blooming sparkle
drapes my hips like
hope of hopscotch
and bangs swept side
ways. A lager of chain
circles my chinbone
like energy from
solar waves shifting.

In that frock I could
spin on one barbed sail,
fight like a banshee without
creasing the bodice,
undress like a lover
in one fell swoop of
of a zipper, pooling
at my feet.

The silk sparkles
at my skin slithers.
Prom blooming agave
at dusk, fleeting feels,
quiet, fled so merry
he mirths me mortar,
lightening bugs of sea,
shuddering sea.

Forbidden Plums...

Or one blossom of Century plant, crashing into sky from its Aloe bed.
A head falling slightly off the edge. There is laughter, vast as an Irish
moor, warm as red dirt in sun. A mug of old-fashioned shaving cream
swallows a brush of fine boar's hair. An escape is made through an
underground tunnel. Two lone bodies funnel into afternoon,
glowing into evening, sharpening to a fixed point. The point is this,
I could have leapt into crematorium blues. I could have ridden all
that way searching, temple my prayers like a ghost in a cranial prison.
I could have culled springtime from that long-shuttered winter.
Then sirens went off. The neighboring hoodlums came rubbing on the
beat of a tin drum carved into a message. A vase of hyacinth fell over with
the weight of limping stems. A long-held privacy was marked for rapture
and an ailing aunt passed quietly into air. She, an unusual child, whose
freckles disarmed the holy gathered held a forbidden plum in her mouth
until a crimped light broke through a small window. You could see one bright
flower in a crib of soft mud, like a solitary cloud wisping for a miracle.

Time, like a River, Flows Away
"Confucius say…"

If you wrote this poem for me,
people on your block could see
the signs before you turned in.

The cat would whine like
a siren taking another neighbor
out on the town, while a loyal

responder would force
quick decisions not even
St. Anthony should have to

endure. St. George, on the flip
side could take out a policy in
the district of Lydda, stand by

his principles, and leave mother
England rapt in his arms. If you
wrote into play fresh mulberries

and cream, I'd pour tea to repay
your kind élan, the candor of your
vision, the dates you make grove.

I'd see myself in your lens. You'd
take them off, fold them over, then
take mine off and lean in closer.

If you wrote this, not me, the mask
of provision would surely provide,
and in a timeless river, flowing.

Our ancestors would bow and cheer,
fold hands together under influence
of Chopin.

Red Feathered Flock
cento: with language from Juanita Davis

The red-whiskered bird came from the dark.
Flitting as if from nowhere to nowhere.

Beneath its own invisible moon, the bird shone
from within. Lonely bird, bird of light prey.

It sang towards a deliciousness without shame, but
the bird made it all up. Fantasia bird. Pirate bird.

Bird of gloss and wisp. Grounded, dreaming of freedom.
A life force that overpowers death. A long-dying fowl.

The graveyards dark monument holds it now, its
dimming luminescence. Feathers dropping like finale, like

an inconclusive fandango. I don't care for wings any longer.
Give me a clean carved scapula, punk rock mantle, and bones.

PAINTED LADIES & PANTS

Silk pillowcase over clouds of buckwheat husk.
Your head props up the night of a new moon,
and I trust in its light, call it sugar bear.
It sends the rainforest to greet its own moss.
The praise comes in without pants, like
a girl I knew in an off-shoulder dream.
Clavicle and kiss on a stairwell, empty
of climbing, fresh fruit at the foot of earth.

Pants should come off at an inkling, then listen
to what trees know without being taught.
The lesson of tree and river flows to us
from the other. It rains like glow worms in
the dark. Your elbow under my neck like
the turn of a century. We have it coming
from what melds golden and storied between
these few lines of verse.

If we keep going like this, the computer is
likely to sell itself short, like a neighbor just
back from the coast where palm fronds nod
to the ocean and six feet apart is just another
way of saying, *nothing can come between us.*

GATHERED SAFELY IN
poem for Perla Batalla

"Dance me through the panic till I'm gathered safely in." —Leonard Cohen

If I end you till the dance of time
Will the dance continue
      Or will time stop it
        Spin retro causation

Take its own sweet punctuation
Mark of a question
      Call me *you*
      By my name-given

The syllables look right past me
      The wrongs number
      The mountains burn

Rage flares
      Masking in the streets
Streets roped off
      Hope loss wrought

If I end you till the dance of time
      Will you ration me like paper
      Will you roast me earthwise

A forest mouthed in honey crisp
      Will the eye of your apple
      Seek early emancipation

What is slavery, after all, if not for cages
What are babies, if not the border of our bodies
      flung wide ajar
      Open Open

What is open, if not action
What is marvel, if not a shift

If I end you till the dance of time
 will we gather safely in?

ABOUT THE AUTHOR

PEGGY DOBREER is the 2021 Honorary Sharon Olds Scholarship Recipient for Community of Writers in the Virtual Valley. She is a Los Angeles poet and writing/meditation mentor whose work has been published in *Moria, Pirene's Fountain, Malpais Review, Everything About You Is Beautiful, San Pedro River Review, Yoga Magazine,* and *Inner Visions* among others. Her work is also included in multiple anthologies, most recently: *Voices From Leimert Park* (Harriet Tubman Press for Tsehai Publishers); *Aeolian Harp Anthology Series Vols. I and V,* (Glass Lyre Press). Dobreer has been nominated twice for a Pushcart Prize and was awarded the 2017 "Poetry Matters Prize" from The Downey Symphony Orchestra in association with NASA. A former choreographer, designer, and lifelong experiential researcher of somatic practice and mystical traditions, Peggy is co-author of "64 Ways to Practice Nonviolence: A Curriculum and Resource Guide," (Pro-Ed Inc.) and was a Program Director at AROHO2015, a women's writing retreat at Ghost Ranch in New Mexico. She is a mother and a member of the Long Now Foundation.

Glass Lyre Press

exceptional works to replenish the spirit

Glass Lyre Press is an independent literary publisher interested in technically accomplished, stylistically distinct, and original work. Glass Lyre seeks diverse writers that possess a dynamic aesthetic and an ability to emotionally and intellectually engage a wide audience of readers.

Glass Lyre's vision is to connect the world through language and art. We hope to expand the scope of poetry and short fiction for the general reader through exceptionally well-written books, which evoke emotion, provide insight, and resonate with the human spirit.

Poetry Collections
Poetry Chapbooks
Select Short & Flash Fiction
Anthologies

www.GlassLyrePress.com

www.ingramcontent.com/pod-product-compliance
Lightning Source LLC
Chambersburg PA
CBHW030201100526
44592CB00009B/392